Shargunam S
Rajakumar G

Introduction to Biometrics and Multimodal Biometric Techniques

Shargunam S
Rajakumar G

Introduction to Biometrics and Multimodal Biometric Techniques

Multimodal Biometrics

Noor Publishing

Imprint
Any brand names and product names mentioned in this book are subject to trademark, brand or patent protection and are trademarks or registered trademarks of their respective holders. The use of brand names, product names, common names, trade names, product descriptions etc. even without a particular marking in this work is in no way to be construed to mean that such names may be regarded as unrestricted in respect of trademark and brand protection legislation and could thus be used by anyone.

Cover image: www.ingimage.com

Publisher:
Noor Publishing
is a trademark of
Dodo Books Indian Ocean Ltd., member of the OmniScriptum S.R.L Publishing group
str. A.Russo 15, of. 61, Chisinau-2068, Republic of Moldova Europe
Printed at: see last page
ISBN: 978-620-3-85754-2

INTRODUCTION TO BIOMETRICS AND MULTIMODAL BIOMETRICS TECHNIQUES

S. Shargunam, Dr. G. Rajakumar

TABLE OF CONTENTS

UNIT-1

INTRODUCTION TO BIOMETRICS

1.1. INTRODUCTION

The expression "biometrics" is gotten from the Greek words bio (life) and metric (to gauge). For our utilization, biometrics alludes to advances for estimating and breaking down an individual's physiological or conduct qualities. These attributes are special to people subsequently can be utilized to confirm or distinguish an individual. Biometrics is the estimation and factual investigation of individuals' extraordinary physical and conduct qualities. The innovation is for the most part utilized for distinguishing proof and access control or for recognizing people who are under reconnaissance. The essential reason of biometric confirmation is that each individual can be precisely distinguished by their natural physical or social characteristics. The term biometrics is derived from the Greek words bio, meaning life, and metric, and meaning to measure.

There are two key words in this definition: "automated" and "person". The word "automated" differentiates biometrics from the larger field of human identification science. Biometric authentication techniques are done completely by machine, generally (but not always) a digital computer. Forensic laboratory techniques, such as latent fingerprint, DNA, hair and fiber analysis, are not considered part of this field. Although automated identification techniques can be used on animals, fruits and vegetables, manufactured goods and the deceased, the subjects of biometric authentication are living humans. For this reason, the field should perhaps be more accurately called "anthropometric authentication". The second key word is "person". Statistical techniques, particularly using fingerprint patterns, have been used to differentiate or connect groups of people or to probabilistically link persons to groups, but biometrics is interested only in recognizing people as individuals. All of the measures used contain both physiological and behavioural components, both of which can vary widely or be quite similar across a population of individuals. No technology is purely one or the other, although some measures seem to be more behaviourally influenced and some more physiologically influenced. The behavioural component of all biometric measures introduces a "human factors" or "psychological" aspect to biometric authentication as well. In practice, we often abbreviate the term "biometric authentication" as "biometrics", although the latter term has been historically used to mean the branch of biology that deals with its data statistically and by quantitative analysis. So "biometrics", in this context, is the use of computers to recognize people, despite all of the across-individual similarities and within-individual variations. Determining "true" identity is beyond the scope of any biometric technology.

Rather, biometric technology can only link a person to a biometric pattern and any identity data (common name) and personal attributes (age, gender, profession, residence, nationality) presented at the time of enrolment in the system. Biometric systems inherently require no identity data, thus allowing anonymous recognition. Ultimately, the performance of a biometric authentication system, and its suitability for any particular task, will depend upon the interaction of individuals with the automated mechanism. It is this interaction of technology with human physiology and psychology that makes "biometrics" such a fascinating subject.

Because biometrics can provide a reasonable level of confidence in authenticating a person with less friction for the user, it has the potential to dramatically improve enterprise security. Computers and devices can unlock automatically when they detect the fingerprints of an approved user. Server room doors can swing open when they recognize the faces of trusted system administrators. Help desk systems might automatically pull up all relevant information when they recognize an employee's voice on the support line.

1.2. HOW BIOMETRICS WORKS

Authentication by biometric verification is becoming increasingly common in corporate and public security systems, consumer electronics and point-of-sale (POS) applications. In addition to security, the driving force behind biometric verification has been convenience, as there are no passwords to remember or security tokens to carry. Some biometric methods, such as measuring a person's gait, can operate with no direct contact with the person being authenticated.

1.3. COMPONENTS

Components of biometric devices include the following:
- a reader or scanning device to record the biometric factor being authenticated;
- software to convert the scanned biometric data into a standardized digital format and to compare match points of the observed data with stored data; and
- A database to securely store biometric data for comparison.

Biometric data may be held in a centralized database, although modern biometric implementations often depend instead on gathering biometric data locally and then cryptographically hashing it so that authentication or identification can be accomplished without direct access to the biometric data itself.

1.4. TYPES OF BIOMETRICS

The two main types of biometric identifiers are either physiological characteristics or behavioural characteristics.

Physiological identifiers relate to the composition of the user being authenticated and include the following:

- facial recognition
- fingerprints
- finger geometry (the size and position of fingers)
- iris recognition
- vein recognition
- retina scanning
- voice recognition
- DNA (deoxyribonucleic acid) matching
- digital signatures

Behavioural identifiers include the unique ways in which individuals act, including recognition of typing patterns, walking gait and other gestures. Some of these behavioural identifiers can be used to provide continuous authentication instead of a single one-off authentication check. Biometric data can be used to access information on a device like a smartphone, but there are also other ways biometrics can be used. For example, biometric information can be held on a smart card, where a recognition system will read an individual's biometric information, while comparing that against the biometric information on the smart card.

As technology improves, the systems are likely to get better at accurately identifying individuals, but less effective at distinguishing between humans and robots. Here are some common approaches:

Typing patterns: Everybody has a different typing style. The speed at which they type, the length of time it takes to go from one letter to another, the degree of impact on the keyboard.

Physical movements: The way that someone walks is unique to an individual and can be used to authenticate employees in a building, or as a secondary layer of authentication for particularly sensitive locations.

Navigation patterns: Mouse movements and finger movements on trackpads or touch-sensitive screens are unique to individuals and relatively easy to detect with software, no additional hardware required.

Engagement patterns: We all interact with technology in different ways. How we open and use apps, how low we allow our battery to get, the locations and times of day we're most likely to use our devices, the way we navigate websites, how we tilt our phones when we hold them, or even how often we check our social media accounts are all potentially unique behavioural characteristics. These behaviour patterns can be used to distinguish people from bots, until the bots get better at imitating humans. And they can also be used in combination with other authentication methods, or, if the technology improves enough, as standalone security measures.

1.5. ADVANTAGES AND DISADVANTAGES OF BIOMETRICS

The use of biometrics has plenty of advantages and disadvantages regarding its use, security and other related functions. Biometrics are beneficial because they are:

- hard to fake or steal, unlike passwords;
- easy and convenient to use;
- generally, the same over the course of a user's life;
- non-transferable; and
- Efficient because templates take up less storage.

Disadvantages, however, include the following:

- It is costly to get a biometric system up and running.
- If the system fails to capture all of the biometric data, it can lead to failure in identifying a user.
- Databases holding biometric data can still be hacked.
- Errors such as false rejects and false accepts can still happen.
- If a user gets injured, then a biometric authentication system may not work -- for example, if a user burns their hand, then a fingerprint scanner may not be able to identify them.

1.6. INSTANCES OF BIOMETRICS BEING USED

Beside biometrics being in a huge number being used today, biometrics are utilized in a wide range of fields. For instance, biometrics are utilized in the accompanying fields and associations:

- **Law implementation.** It is utilized in frameworks for criminal IDs, for example, finger impression or palm print verification frameworks.

- **The United States Department of Homeland Security.** It is utilized in Border Patrol branches for various identification, confirming and credentialing measures - for instance, with frameworks for electronic travel papers, which store unique finger impression information, or in facial acknowledgment frameworks.

- **Medical services.** It is utilized in frameworks, for example, public character cards for ID and health care coverage programs, which may utilize fingerprints for recognizable proof.

- **Air terminal security.** This field now and then uses biometrics like iris acknowledgment.

Be that as it may, not all associations and projects will select in to utilizing biometrics. For instance, some equity frameworks won't utilize biometrics so they can keep away from any conceivable blunder that may happen.

1.7. SECURITY AND PROTECTION ISSUES OF BIOMETRICS

Biometric identifiers rely upon the uniqueness of the factor being thought of. For instance, fingerprints are for the most part viewed as profoundly extraordinary to every individual. Finger impression acknowledgment, particularly as carried out in Apple's Touch ID for past iPhones, was the principal broadly utilized mass-market utilization of a biometric verification factor. Other biometric factors incorporate retina, iris acknowledgment, vein and voice examines. Nonetheless, they have not been received broadly up until this point, in some part, on the grounds that there is less trust in the uniqueness of the identifiers or in light of the fact that the elements are simpler to farce and use for pernicious reasons, similar to wholesale fraud. Strength of the biometric factor can likewise be imperative to acknowledgment of the factor. Fingerprints don't change over a long period, while facial appearance can change definitely with age, sickness or different variables.

The main protection issue of utilizing biometrics is that actual qualities, similar to fingerprints and retinal vein designs, are by and large static and can't be altered. This is unmistakable from no biometric factors, similar to passwords (something one knows) and tokens (something one has), which can be supplanted on the off chance that they are penetrated or in any case undermined. A showing of this trouble was the more than 20 million people whose fingerprints were undermined in the 2014 U.S. Office of Personnel Management (OPM) information break. The expanding universality of top notch cameras, mouthpieces and unique finger impression perusers in large numbers of the present cell phones implies biometrics will keep on turning into a more normal technique for confirming clients, especially as Fast ID Online (FIDO) has determined new principles for verification with biometrics that help two-factor confirmation (2FA) with biometric factors. While the nature of biometric peruses keeps on improving, they can in any case deliver bogus negatives, when an approved client isn't perceived or confirmed, and bogus positives, when an unapproved client is perceived and verified.

Three Types of Biometrics Security

While they can have other applications, biometrics have been often used in security, and you can mostly label biometrics into three groups:

1. Biological biometrics
2. Morphological biometrics
3. Behavioral biometrics

- **Biological biometrics** use traits at a genetic and molecular level. These may include features like DNA or your blood, which might be assessed through a sample of your body's fluids.
- **Morphological biometrics** involve the structure of your body. More physical traits like your eye, fingerprint, or the shape of your face can be mapped for use with security scanners.
- **Behavioral biometrics** are based on patterns unique to each person. How you walk, speak, or even type on a keyboard can be an indication of your identity if these patterns are tracked.

Biometric identification has a growing role in our everyday security. Physical characteristics are relatively fixed and individualized — even in the case of twins. Each person's unique biometric identity can be used to replace or at least augment password systems for computers, phones, and restricted access rooms and buildings.

Once biometric data is obtained and mapped, it is then saved to be matched with future attempts at access. Most of the time, this data is encrypted and stored within the device or in a remote server.

Biometrics scanners are hardware used to capture the biometric for verification of identity. These scans match against the saved database to approve or deny access to the system.

In other words, biometric security means your body becomes the "key" to unlock your access. Biometrics are largely used because of two major benefits:

- Convenience of use: Biometrics are always with you and cannot be lost or forgotten.
- Difficult to steal or impersonate: Biometrics can't be stolen like a password or key can.
- While these systems are not perfect, they offer tons of promise for the future of cybersecurity.

1.8. BIOMETRIC WEAKNESSES AND RELIABILITY

While excellent cameras and different sensors help empower the utilization of biometrics, they can likewise empower assailants. Since individuals don't protect their faces, ears, hands, voice or step, assaults are conceivable basically by catching biometric information from individuals without their assent or information. An early assault on unique mark biometric validation was known as the sticky bear hack, and it traces all the way back to 2002 when Japanese specialists, utilizing a gelatin-based dessert, showed that an aggressor could lift an inactive finger impression from a gleaming surface; the capacitance of gelatin is like that of a human finger, so finger impression scanners intended to distinguish capacitance would be tricked by the gelatin move.

Decided assailants can likewise crush other biometric factors. In 2015, Jan Krissler, otherwise called Starbug, a Chaos Computer Club biometrics analyst, exhibited a strategy for extricating sufficient information from a high-goal photo to overcome iris filtering validation. In 2017, Krissler revealed crushing the iris scanner validation plot utilized by the Samsung Galaxy S8 cell phone. Krissler had recently reproduced a client's thumbprint from a high-goal picture to exhibit that Apple's Touch ID fingerprinting validation plot was additionally helpless. After Apple delivered iPhone X, it took analysts only fourteen days to sidestep Apple's Face ID facial acknowledgment utilizing a 3D-printed veil; Face ID can likewise be crushed by people identified with the validated client, including kids or kin.

Phones, company servers, and the applications used to test them may all leak authentication credentials such as fingerprint scans or voice recordings. False positives and false negatives are also a real possibility. A person who is wearing makeup or glasses, or who is sick or tired, may be missed by a facial recognition device. Voices differ as well.

When people first wake up, or when they want to use their phone in a busy public space, or when they're frustrated or impatient, they sound different. Masks, images and voice records, copies of fingerprints, and trusted family members or housemates can all be used to fool recognition systems when the legitimate user is sleeping.

Companies can use several forms of authentication at the same time, according to experts, and escalate rapidly if they see warning signs. If the fingerprint matches but not the face, or if the account is accessed from an unusual location at an unusual time, it could be time to turn to a backup authentication system or a secondary communication channel. This is especially important.

1.9. HOW SECURE IS BIOMETRIC AUTHENTICATION DATA?

The security of the biometric confirmation information is indispensably significant, considerably more than the security of passwords, since passwords can be effectively changed in the event that they are uncovered. A unique finger impression or retinal sweep, in any case, is unchanging. The arrival of this or other biometric data could put clients at lasting danger and make critical legitimate openness for the organization that loses the information.

"In case of a penetrate, it makes a Herculean test on the grounds that actual attributions, for example, fingerprints can't be supplanted," says information security master Kon Leong, CEO and prime supporter at San Jose-based ZL Technologies. "Biometric information in the possession of a bad element, maybe an administration, conveys terrifying however genuine ramifications also. "

By the day's end, each organization is liable for its own security choices. You can't reevaluate consistence, yet you can lessen the expense of consistence, and the potential repercussions of a hole, by picking the correct merchant. On the off chance that a little or fair sized organization utilizes, say, Google's or Apple's confirmation innovation and there's a security break with Google or Apple, it's probably Google or Apple will get the fault.

Also, organizations that don't keep certifications on document have some lawful assurances. For instance, numerous retailers can stay away from considerable consistence costs by keeping their frameworks "out of degree." Payment data is encoded directly at the installment terminal and goes straight through to an installment processor. Crude installment card information never contacts the organization workers, decreasing both consistence suggestions and potential security hazards.

On the off chance that an organization needs to gather confirmation data and keep it on its own workers, best-practice safety efforts ought to be applied. That incorporates encryption both for information very still and information on the way. New advances are accessible for runtime encryption, which keeps the information in scrambled structure even while it is being utilized.

Encryption is certifiably not an undeniable certainty of safety, obviously, if the applications or clients that are approved to get to the information are themselves bargained. Notwithstanding, there two or three different ways that organizations can try not to keep even encoded verification information on their workers.

1.10. PRIVACY RISKS OF BIOMETRIC AUTHENTICATION?

A few clients probably won't need organizations gathering information about, say, the hour of day and the areas where they normally utilize their telephones. In the event that this data gets out, it might actually be utilized by stalkers or, on account of VIPs, by sensationalist writers. A few clients probably won't need their relatives or mates to know where they are constantly.

The data could likewise be mishandled by oppressive government systems or criminal examiners exceeding limits. Unfamiliar forces may utilize the data trying to impact general assessment. Dishonest advertisers and promoters may do similarly. A year ago, a wellness application was found to gather data about client areas and uncovering it such that uncovered the area of mystery U.S. army installations and watch courses.

Any of these circumstances might actually prompt critical public shame for the organization that gathered the information, administrative fines, or legal claims. In the event that DNA checks become inescapable, they bring about a totally different space of security concerns such including openness of ailments and family connections.

UNIT-2

FUNDAMENTALS OF BIOMETRIC TECHNOLOGY

This section presents the fundamental idea of the biometric validation innovation. This part is coordinated as follows. Areas 2.1 and 2.2 will give the meaning of biometric innovation and some significant applications. The diverse activity methods of a biometric framework will be examined in Section 2.3. The idea of biometric information ordering will be given in Section 2.4. The various measurements for a biometric framework are characterized in Section 2.5. A concise outline of the diverse biometric modalities will be introduced in Section 2.6.

2.1. BIOMETRIC AUTHENTICATION TECHNOLOGY

Confirmation assumes the urgent part in any security related applications, for example, web based business, safeguard, and so forth In such manner, the biometric is considered lately. Biometrics (old Greek: profiles ="life", metron ="measure") is the investigation of techniques for remarkably perceiving people dependent on at least one natural physiological or conduct qualities of a human. Programmed biometric handling frameworks work by first catching an example of a biometric include, like account an advanced sound sign for voice acknowledgment, or taking a computerized shading picture for face acknowledgment. The example is then changed utilizing a type of numerical capacity onto a biometric layout. The biometric layout gives a standardized and exceptionally segregating portrayal of the element, which would then be able to be equitably contrasted with different formats all together with decide the character of a human. Unique mark, iris, face, hand-calculation, palmprint and ear are the most regularly utilized physiological biometric characteristics, while voice, signature, keystroke elements, stride are the some illustration of social biometric qualities. Figure 2.1 shows the diverse biometric characteristics for an individual. A decent biometric is described by 1) utilization of an element which ought to be exceptionally special so the possibility of any two individuals having a similar list of capabilities is zero, 2) stable so the highlights don't change over the long run, 3) effectively capturable so it is advantageous to the clients and 4) forestalls treating or replicating of highlights.

At the point when a solitary biometric quality is utilized for confirmation reason, at that point the validation framework is called unimodal verification framework. Unimodal biometric frameworks have a few limits like uproarious information, intra-class varieties, and confined levels of opportunity, non-comprehensiveness, parody assaults and unsatisfactory mistake rates. A portion of these impediments can be overwhelmed by utilizing numerous biometric attributes or different

10

wellspring of data. Such framework is called multimodal verification framework. In the various applications, biometrics are utilized in the various modes which are portrayed in the accompanying.

2.2. BIOMETRIC APPLICATIONS

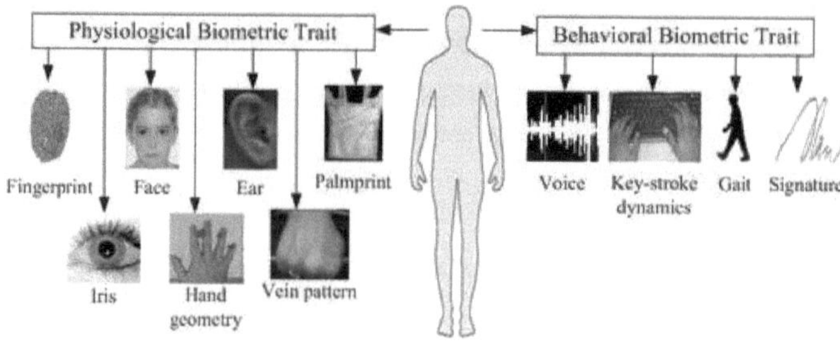

Figure 2.1 Examples of biometric traits that can be used for authenticating an individual. Physical traits include fingerprint, iris, face and hand geometry while behavioural traits include signature, keystroke dynamics and gait.

2.3. OPERATIONAL PROCESS

Depending on the context of applications, a biometric system can operate either in verification or identification mode. In both modes, users have to enroll via enrollment process. The system validates an individual's identity by comparing the captured biometric data with his/her own biometric template(s) stored in the system database in the verification mode. Here, an individual submits a claimed identity to the system, such as personal identification number (PIN), a user name or a smart card. The system performs one-to-one comparisons to determine whether the identity claimed by the individual is genuine or false. In the identification mode, an individual is recognized by searching the templates of all users in the database. In these block diagrams, sensor module captures the raw biometric information from human bodies and feature extraction module processes the raw biometric information and extracts the features which is also referred as biometric template. The matching module compares the templates of two persons and generates a score value which represents the similarity (dissimilarity) of two persons. Finally, the decision module determines the genuineness or the identity of a person in verification or identification mode, respectively.

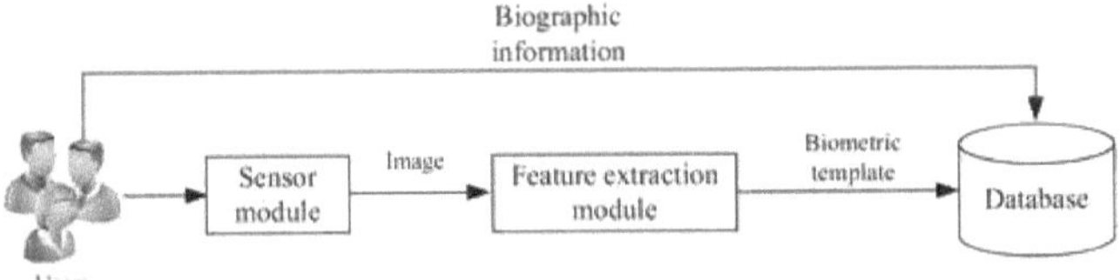

(a) Enrollment steps of an authentication system.

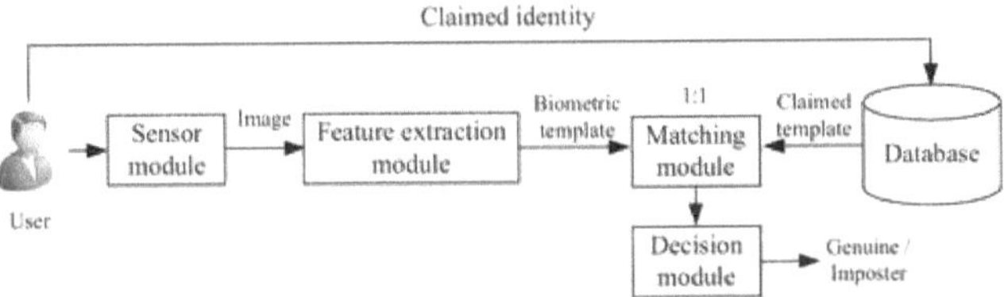

(b) Steps of an authentication system in verification mode

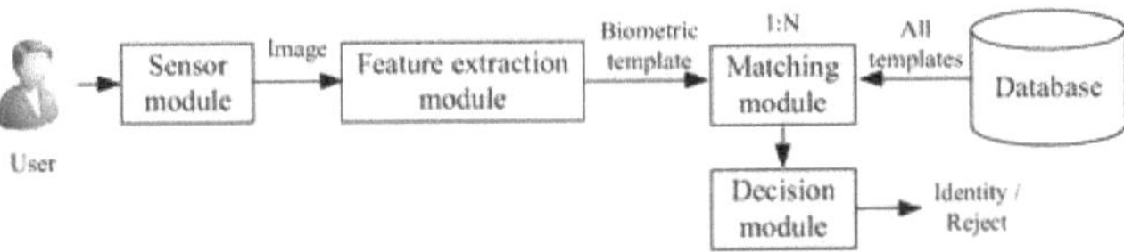

(c) Steps of an authentication system in identification mode

Figure 2.2 Different modes of operations of a biometric authentication system

Moreover, in identification mode, the matching module compares the biometric template of a person with all stored templates in the database. This process is computationally expensive when the number of stored templates in the database is huge. Identification of a person can be done faster if we filter out some templates which are not similar to the captured template.

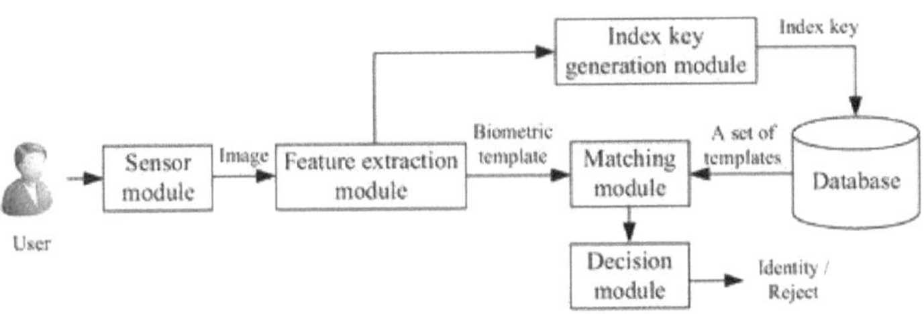

Figure 2.3 Major steps in identification system with indexing.

Biometric information ordering is a plan to create a file key from the biometric information and relegate the way in to the relating format. In view of the file keys the biometric layouts can be arranged into various gatherings in the data set. The ordering method is utilized to proclaim an individual's personality with lesser number of examinations as opposed to looking through the whole information base. An ID framework recovers a little arrangement of comparative formats from the data set dependent on the record key and performs point by point coordinating with the recovered layouts to decide the character of a person. An outline of a recognizable proof framework with ordering is appeared in Fig. 2.3.

2.4. METRICS FOR PERFORMANCE MEASURE

There are a number of performance evaluation metrics followed in biometric authentication system to evaluate the performance. Commonly adopted performance evaluation metrics are stated in the following.

- Genuine Accept Rate (GAR): It is the ratio of the number of input samples correctly classified as genuine to the total number of genuine input samples. A higher value of GAR indicates better performance.

- **Genuine Reject Rate (GRR):** It is the ratio of the number of input samples correctly classified as impostor to the total number of impostor input samples. A higher value of GRR indicates better performance.

- **False Accept Rate (FAR):** It is the proportion of impostor input samples falsely classified as genuine samples. It may be noted that $FAR = 1 - GRR$. A lower value of FAR indicates a better performance of a system.

- **False Reject Rate (FRR):** It is the proportion of number of genuine input samples falsely classified as impostor samples. Please note that $F\,RR = 1 - GAR$. A lower value of F RR indicates a better performance of a biometric authentication system.

- **Equal Error Rate (ERR):** When FRR becomes equal to FAR, the ratio is called as equal error rate. A lower value of ERR indicates a better performance.

- **Failure To Acquire (FTA) or Failure To Capture (FTC):** It is the ratio of the number of times a biometric system fails to capture the biometric sample presented to it. A lower value of F T A indicates better acquisition performance.

- **Failure To Enroll (FTE):** It is the ratio of the number of users that cannot be successfully enrolled into a biometric system to a total number of users presented to the biometric system. A lower value of F T E indicates better population coverage.

2.5. LOCAL OR DEVICE-BASED AUTHENTICATION

The most widely recognized illustration of a nearby validation system is the equipment security module in a cell phone. Client data —, for example, a unique finger impression filter, facial picture or a voice print — is put away inside the module. At the point when confirmation is required, biometric data is gathered by the unique finger impression per user, camera or amplifier and shipped off the module where it's contrasted with the first. The module tells the telephone whether the new data is a match to what it previously had put away.

With this framework, the crude biometric data is never open to any product or framework outside the module, including the telephone's own working framework. On the iPhone, this is known as the safe territory and is accessible on each telephone with an Apple A7 chip or more current. The primary telephone with this innovation was the iPhone 5S, delivered in 2013. Comparative innovation is additionally accessible on Android telephones. Samsung, for instance, begun carrying out the ARM TrustZone confided in execution climate with the Samsung S3 cell phone.

Today, cell phone equipment security modules are utilized to give security to Apple Pay, Google Pay and Samsung Pay just as to confirm outsider applications. PayPal, for instance, can utilize a telephone's biometric sensor for confirmation without PayPal truly seeing the genuine biometric information itself. Square Cash, Venmo, Dropbox and many banking applications and secret key administration applications influence this validation system also.

Undertakings can likewise utilize cell phone based biometric perusers at whatever point their clients or clients approach cell phones, while never gathering and store any recognizing biometric data on their own workers. Comparable innovation is accessible for different kinds of gadgets, like brilliant cards, keen entryway bolts, or finger impression scanners for PCs.

As per Spiceworks, telephone based finger impression acknowledgment is the most widely recognized biometric verification component being used today. 34% of organizations utilize Apple's Touch ID unique finger impression sensor. Moreover, 14% of organizations use Apple Face ID and 7 percent use Android Face Unlock.

Cell phone based validation offers huge ease of use benefits. To start with, clients will in general be quickly mindful in the event that they have lost or lost their cell phone and will find prompt ways to discover or supplant it. Assuming, notwithstanding, they lose an identification that they just use to get to a structure during the off-hours, they probably won't see for some time that it is absent.

Cell phone producers are likewise in the center of a weapons contest to improve their innovation and simpler to utilize. No other industry — or singular organization — can coordinate with the size of versatile speculation or the convenience and security testing that telephones get.

At long last, telephone validation offers clients greatest adaptability. They can pick telephones with face ID, unique finger impression scanners or voice acknowledgment, or some other new innovation that hasn't been concocted at this point however will overwhelm the market tomorrow. In any case, utilizing an outsider system like buyer cell phones puts the verification interaction outside big business control.

Another drawback to gadget based verification, as a rule, is that the personality data is restricted to that one gadget. Assuming individuals utilize a unique mark to open their cell phone, they can't likewise utilize that equivalent finger impression to open their office entryway without independently approving the entryway lock, or to open their PC without independently approving their PC's finger impression scanner.

Organizations that need to verify clients or clients on numerous gadgets in different areas need to either have some sort of concentrated instrument to store the validation certifications or influence a gadget that the client conveys with them consistently. For instance, organizations can put the verification component inside a keen identification that representatives wear around the workplace. They can likewise utilize a cell phone to validate the worker, at that point impart the personality affirmation to different gadgets and frameworks through Bluetooth, NFC, WiFi or the web.

2.6. TOKENIZATION OR ENCRYPTION

Another way to deal with permitting new gadgets to perceive existing approved clients is tokenization, single direction encryption, or hashing capacities. Say, for instance, retinal, voice or unique mark ID is utilized to perceive and validate workers any place they may go inside an organization, however the organization would not like to have the picture or sound documents put away on workers where programmers or malevolent representatives may abuse them.

All things being equal, the organization would utilize a gadget that, say, filters an individual's face or finger impression, changes over that picture into a one of a kind code, at that point sends that code to the focal worker for validation. Any gadget that utilizes a similar change strategy would then have the option to perceive the worker, and the crude ID information is never accessible on any framework. The disadvantage to this methodology is that the organization is then secured in a solitary exclusive verification component.

UNIT-3

MULTIMODAL BIOMETRIC AND FUSION TECHNOLOGY

3.1 WHY MULTIMODAL BIOMETRICS IS REQUIRED?

The unimodal systems have to deal with various challenges such as lack of secrecy, non-universality of samples, extent of user's comfort and freedom while dealing with the system, spoofing attacks on stored data, etc.

Some of these challenges can be addressed by employing a multimodal biometric system. There are several more reasons for its requirement, such as

- Availability of multiple traits makes the multimodal system more reliable.
- A multimodal biometric system increases security and secrecy of user data.
- A multimodal biometric system conducts fusion strategies to combine decisions from each subsystem and then comes up with a conclusion. This makes a multimodal system more accurate.
- If any of the identifiers fail to work for known or unknown reasons, the system still can provide security by employing the other identifier.
- Multimodal systems can provide knowledge about "liveliness" of the sample being entered by applying liveliness detection techniques. This makes them capable to detect and handle spoofing.

3.2. WORKING OF MULTIMODAL BIOMETRIC SYSTEM

Multimodal biometric system has all the conventional modules a unimodal system has −

- Capturing module
- Feature extraction module
- Comparison module
- Decision making module

In addition, it has a fusion technique to integrate the information from two different authentication systems. The fusion can be done at any of the following levels −

- During feature extraction.

- During comparison of live samples with stored biometric templates.

- During decision making.

The multimodal biometric systems that integrate or fuse the information at initial stage are considered to be more effective than the systems those integrate the information at the later stages. The obvious reason to this is, the early stage contains more accurate information than the matching scores of the comparison modules.

Fusion Scenarios in Multimodal Biometric System

Within a multimodal biometric system, there can be variety in number of traits and components. They can be as follows

- Single biometric trait, multiple sensors.

- Single biometric trait, multiple classifiers (say, minutiae-based matcher and texture-based matcher).

- Single biometric trait, multiple units (say, multiple fingers).

- Multiple biometric traits of an individual (say, iris, fingerprint, etc.).

- These traits are then operated upon to confirm user's identity.

3.3. DESIGN ISSUES WITH MULTIMODAL BIOMETRIC SYSTEMS

You need to consider a number of factors while designing a multimodal biometric system –

- Level of security you need to bring in.

- The number of users who will use the system.

- Types of biometric traits you need to acquire.

- The number of biometric traits from the users.

- The level at which multiple biometric traits need integration.

- The technique to be adopted to integrate the information.

- The trade-off between development cost versus system performance.

3.4. MULTIMODAL BIOMETRIC AUTHENTICATION TECHNOLOGY

In multimodal biometric verification, different modalities are utilized for individual ID. At least two biometric qualities are accumulated from an individual and are utilized to distinguish him/her interestingly. The client is approached to introduce numerous examples for distinguishing proof and the last acknowledgment choice is made on all or a mix of them.

Utilization of more than one methodology enjoys numerous benefits just as difficulties related with it. Modalities, for example, iris and finger impression are extraordinary and exact and assume a significant part in the general dynamic interaction. Utilization of numerous modalities permits more clients to take on the framework since they can introduce substitute modalities if the ones requested are not adequate at that point because of a sickness, a physical issue or some other troubles. Multimodality additionally makes it progressively hard to counterfeit different modalities. The exactness of unimodal frameworks is unfavourably influenced by the information test quality. Utilization of various modalities gives strength against test quality debasement. It likewise assists with improving the unwavering quality of a biometric framework.

While planning a multimodal biometric framework, one should believe the kind of information to be gained (e.g.. 2 Dimensional or 3 Dimensional), the sort of acknowledgment calculation to be utilized on every information component (for example Head Component Analysis (PCA) or Independent Component Analysis (ICA)), the yield of a calculation (the distance or mistake metric), how to consolidate them and the level at which it ought to be performed. All these are the significant difficulties in multimodal biometric verification framework.

3.5. FUSION OF MULTIMODALITIES

Compared to a unimodal biometric authentication system, a multimodal system requires more storage space to store the different types of samples. The benefits of a multimodal system may get overshadowed if it takes inordinate amounts of storage space and consequently increasing times for sample collection, templates matching and decision making. To overcome these limitations, a possible approach is to combine multiple modalities. This approach is called as fusion. The fusion can be performed at various stages in a biometric authentication system. These stages are called fusion levels.

- **Sensor Level Fusion**: In sensor level fusion, outputs of the different sensors are fused together to form a new input which is used in further stages.

- **Feature Level Fusion:** Features extracted from the different biometric modalities are combined to form a single feature vector in this level of fusion.

- **Match-score Level Fusion:** After comparing the stored template and query sample the matcher produces a measure of their similarity called as a match score. The match score produced by the different matchers are combined in this level of fusion.

- **Decision Level Fusion:** The decisions made by the different matchers are combined in this level of fusion to arrive at the final recognition decision.

The fusion techniques help in reducing the total number of feature vectors from the different modalities which otherwise would have increased the storage space requirements manifolds. Taking the specialist capabilities of each classifier, a combined classifier may be build up to provide better results than a single classifier. In other words, combining the different expert's results in a system can outperform the experts when taken individually. This is especially true if the different experts are not correlated. It also increases the degrees of freedom. The concern of time spent in processing of multiple modalities can be avoided by use of parallel mode of operations.

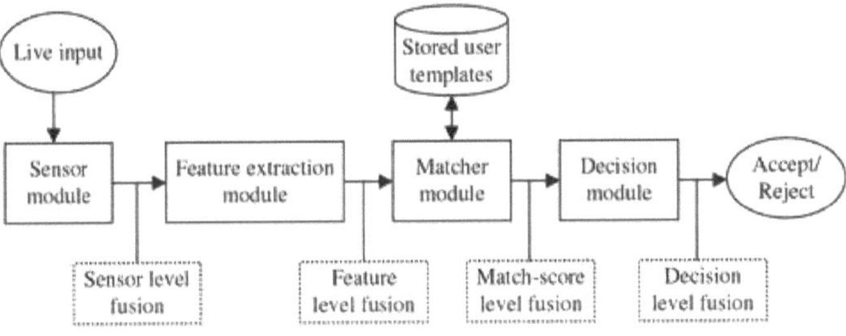

Figure 3.1 Block diagram of the different levels of fusion.

3.6. FUSION LEVELS

This section will talk about various levels of fusion. A typical biometric system is shown in Fig. 3.1 with the sensor, feature extraction, matcher and decision making modules. Each modality requires a separate set of these four modules. Information available at the output of each of these modules can then be combined and passed onto the next module. This process of combining information is known as fusion. Fusion can be carried out at four different places or levels as shown in Fig. 3.1. A brief description about each level of fusion, the issues that are required to be handled in order to fuse information at these levels, the limitations of information fusion at those levels and their advantages and disadvantages are presented in the following.

3.6.1 Sensor Level Fusion

Sensor level combination is combination performed at the soonest stage and is done before the component extraction stage. The sensors catch a biometric attribute like facial picture, iris picture, unique finger impression and so forth the principle objective of the sensor level combination is to intertwine these caught tests as they contain the most extravagant measure of data about that biometric quality.

Issues in Sensor Level Fusion: Typically, sensor level combination should be possible if the examples address the equivalent biometric quality. For example, numerous previews of a face can be taken by cameras situated at the various areas and are then consolidated to frame a composite 3D picture. Sensor level combination is more gainful and valuable in multi-test frameworks where numerous examples of an equivalent biometric attribute are taken and consolidated to shape a composite example. The examples to be melded should be viable. Existing Approaches to Sensor Level Fusion: Sensor level combination includes the arrangement of a composite picture or sign. A 3D face picture can be produced from numerous perspectives on similar face in two measurements of fingerprints is acted to shape a composite finger impression from various spot prints. The client gives different touch prints of his unique mark and they are consolidated to frame a finger impression mosaic and utilized numerous 2D pictures of human face alongside infrared and 3D pictures of something similar. These pictures are utilized in seven distinct mixes going from the individual pictures to each of the three sorts of pictures and the test results show the 2D+3D+infrared blend delivers the littlest EER of under 0.002%. All in all, the multi-test combination of facial pictures gives the most exact acknowledgment execution as analyzed that of the individual pictures.

Benefits: As the sensor yields contain crude information, the data content is the most extravagant at this degree of combination. A particularly rich measure of information can contain commotion which might be because of improper lighting conditions, foundation clamor, and presence of soil and sweat on the sensor surface. Clamor decreases the nature of a biometric test and will debase the exactness of the confirmation framework however the lavishness of data accessible at this level takes into consideration use of test quality improvement strategies without the deficiency of any data. Crude information is additionally the biggest in size and combination of such information decreases the absolute required extra room.

Constraints: Sensor level combination is material just to multi-occurrence and multi-test biometric frameworks which contain various examples or tests of the equivalent biometric characteristic. Multimodal biometric frameworks require tests from the various modalities to be joined. Tests from the various modalities may not be viable and thus can't be utilized for sensor level combination. A large portion of the business off-the-rack (COTS) items don't give sensor yields. Performing sensor level combination all things considered is absurd.

3.6.2 Feature Level Fusion

This is the second degree of data combination in a biometric validation framework. The component extraction stage produces include vectors which contain the second most extravagant degree of data when contrasted with the crude information caught by biometric sensors. Putting away element vectors rather than crude information requires similarly less extra room. Yet at the same time, these element vectors are high dimensional and to store such high dimensional component vectors from the various modalities more space is needed than that for a solitary methodology. Basic strategies like averaging or weighted averaging, include level combination can be utilized to decrease the complete number of highlight vectors in the event that they begin from a similar component extraction calculation.

Issues in highlight level combination: Feature sets of the various modalities are by and large not viable as every methodology has its own one of a kind highlights (for example fingerprints contain minutia focuses which are characterized by their sort and direction though irises are distinguished by their example and shading data which are scalar substances). This kind of combination strategies can be applied just when the capabilities are viable or potentially firmly synchronized. Modalities like hand math and palmprint or voice and comparing lip and facial developments are firmly coupled modalities and can be synchronized by combination at this level. Biometric frameworks that utilization include level combination may experience the ill effects of the scourge of dimensionality on the off chance that they utilize straightforward link of highlight vectors as a combination method.

Existing ways to deal with highlight level combination: Feature level combination is for the most part accomplished by link of highlight vectors. Highlight vectors acquired from the element extraction phases of the various modalities are just connected to frame the resultant element vector which might be in higher measurements than any of its constituent vectors and propose a novel way to deal with highlight level combination of ear and face profile utilizing Kernel Canonical Correlation Analysis (KCCA) first guide the element vectors into a higher dimensional space prior to applying relationship investigation on them.

Benefits: Feature vectors contain second most extravagant degree of data when contrasted with the crude biometric information. Highlight level combination takes into account synchronization of firmly coupled modalities like face and lip developments while talking or modalities like hand math and palmprint. This synchronization can turn away parody assaults as faking facial developments just as voice precisely simultaneously isn't simple. It can likewise be utilized as a vivacity recognition procedure.

Limits: Methods like connection are by and large utilized for joining highlight vectors. Such a connection brings about an expansion in the absolute number of vector measurements and the framework may experience the ill effects of revile of dimensionality and accordingly, debased acknowledgment execution. Putting away an ale dimensional element vector additionally occupies important extra space. Highlight link likewise brings about the clamor from the melded modalities getting accumulated too. Commotion lessens the nature of a biometric test caught and will debase the exactness of the validation framework. The vast majority of the business off-the-rack () items don't give highlight vectors. Playing out an element level combination all things considered is unimaginable.

3.6.3   Match Score Level Fusion

Match score level combination is level three of combination in a normal biometric verification framework. The biometric matcher module produces match scores which are a pointer of similitude or uniqueness between the information test and the one put away in a data set. Match scores establish the third most extravagant degree of data after crude information and highlight vectors and match score level combination targets joining these match scores and utilize the resultant score to settle on a last acknowledgment choice. As these scores are promptly accessible, match score level combination is the best degree of combination.

Issues in match-score level combination: Not all biometric matchers yield their scores in a fixed arrangement. Some biometric matchers may yield similitude scores while others may give difference scores. The scores may even follow the diverse mathematical reaches and circulations. These scores are needed to fall in a typical mathematical reach and standardization methods are utilized to accomplish that. An itemized investigation of standardization strategies.

Existing methodologies for match-score level combination: Score level combination is the most famous degree of combination and many examination works are committed to it. When the scores are standardized, straightforward number juggling rules like aggregate, weighted whole, item, weighted item, result of probabilities, amount of probabilities, min-max score can be utilized. Procedures like matcher weighting and client weighting are investigated. Matcher weighting procedures allocate loads to the matchers dependent on the precision of that biometric attribute. While the client weighting strategies allocate client explicit loads to every client. These loads are resolved experimentally.

Benefits: Commercial-off-the-rack (COTS) items offer admittance to the match scores subsequently, they are promptly accessible for combination. Match scores are basic genuine numbers inside a specific numeric reach and along these lines can go through any mathematical changes. They likewise contain the most minimal degree of information intricacy. This makes them both more clearly and consolidate. Match scores are the littlest in size contrasted with the crude information and highlight vector.

Limits: Match scores are needed to be standardized before combination. The vigor of standardization strategies assumes a significant part in the heartiness of the biometric framework that utilizes it.

3.6.4   Decision Level Fusion

This is the fourth degree of data combination in a biometric confirmation framework. Test for each biometric quality goes through the different sensor, include extraction and coordinating with modules. The matchers settle on an autonomous neighbourhood choice about the character of a client. Choice level combination targets melding these neighbourhood choices to shape a last/worldwide acknowledgment choice that groups the client as real or an impostor.

Issues in choice level combination: This is the most un-rich degree of data as the measure of data accessible for combination can be a basic paired 0s and 1s (1 showing a match and 0 demonstrating a non-match) or match/non-match drawstring.. Since an official conclusion is made on a specific blend of the choices yield by the various matchers, their setups; successive or equal, assumes a significant part in the development of a ultimate choice just as the degree of safety given by the framework.

Existing ways to deal with choice level combination: Existing methodologies comprise of straightforward standards like the AND rule, the OR rule dominant part and weighted lion's share casting a ballot. Bayesian combination rules are likewise utilized which target changing the choice names yield by singular matchers into likelihood esteems. Conduct information space technique is a strategy for choice level combination which utilizes a look-into table to choose the last name dependent on the names yield by singular matchers.

Benefits: Fusion of choices takes into consideration the utilization of free, unimodal biometric confirmation items off the rack. Items from the various sellers can likewise be utilized without agonizing over their similarity. Additionally the security level of the whole framework can be changed according to the necessity by changing the arrangement where the matchers are associated. Choice level combination utilizes the littlest and the most unambiguous snippet of data for combination for example the matcher choice. As the most business off-the-rack items (COTS) give admittance to just a ultimate conclusion, make this as the lone conceivable and doable degree of combination.

Restrictions: Relative exhibitions of the matchers should be contemplated while settling on a ultimate choice. Weighted combination rules should allocate matcher loads dependent on the overall precision of the matchers, with the goal that the most exact matcher assumes a significant part in deciding an ultimate choice.

3.7. CRITERIA FOR EFFECTIVE BIOMETRIC SYSTEM

There are seven basic criteria for measuring effectiveness of a biometric system

- Uniqueness – It determines how uniquely a biometric system can recognize a user from a group of users. It is a primary criterion.

- Universality – It indicates requirement for unique characteristics of each person in the world, which cannot be reproduced. It is a secondary criterion.

- Permanence – It indicates that a personal trait recorded needs to be constant in the database for a certain time period.

- Collectability – It is the ease at which a person's trait can be acquired, measured, or processed further.

- Performance – It is the efficiency of system in terms of accuracy, speed, fault handling, and robustness.

- Acceptability – It is the user-friendliness, or how good the users accept the technology such that they are cooperative to let their biometric trait captured and assessed.

- Circumvention – It is the ease with which a trait is possibly imitated using an artifacts or substitute.

UNIT-4

PATTERN RECOGNITION AND BIOMETRICS

4.1 OVERVIEW

Pattern recognition is the process of recognising and verifying a pattern. A fingerprint picture, a handwritten cursive word, a human face, a speech signal, a bar code, or a web page on the Internet are all examples of patterns.

Person habits are often classified into different groups based on their characteristics. When patterns with similar properties are combined, the resulting gro up is also a pattern, which is often called a pattern class.

Pattern recognition is the science for observing, distinguishing the patterns of interest, and making correct decisions about the patterns or pattern classes. Thus, a biometric system applies pattern recognition to identify and classify the individuals, by comparing it with the stored templates.

4.2 PATTERN RECOGNITION IN BIOMETRICS

The pattern recognition technique conducts the following tasks −

- Classification − Identifying handwritten characters, CAPTCHAs, distinguishing humans from computers.
- Segmentation − Detecting text regions or face regions in images.
- Syntactic Pattern Recognition − Determining how a group of math symbols or operators are related, and how they form a meaningful expression.

4.3 COMPONENTS OF PATTERN RECOGNITION

Pattern recognition technique extracts a random pattern of human trait into a compact digital signature, which can serve as a biological identifier. The biometric systems use pattern recognition techniques to classify the users and identify them separately.

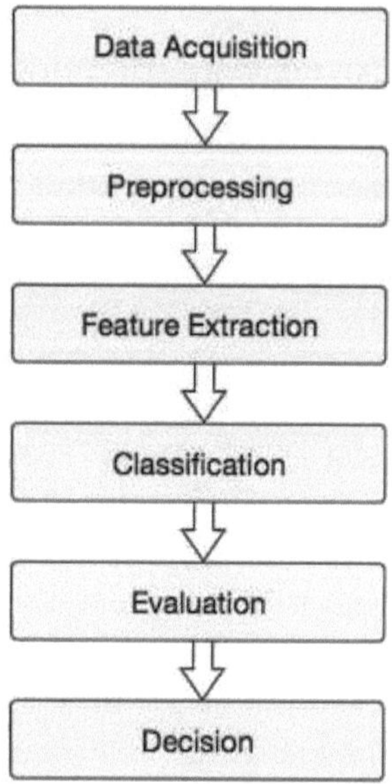

Figure 4.1 Block diagram of the different levels of fusion.

4.4 POPULAR ALGORITHMS IN PATTERN RECOGNITION

The most popular pattern generation algorithms are
- Nearest Neighbour Algorithm

You need to take the unknown individual's vector and compute its distance from all the patterns in the database. The smallest distance gives the best match.
- Back-Propagation (Backprop) Algorithm

It is a bit complex but very useful algorithm that involves a lot of mathematical computations

There are three different forms of vein pattern recognition: palm vein pattern recognition, finger vein pattern recognition (both of which work using near-infrared* light) and retina vein pattern recognition.

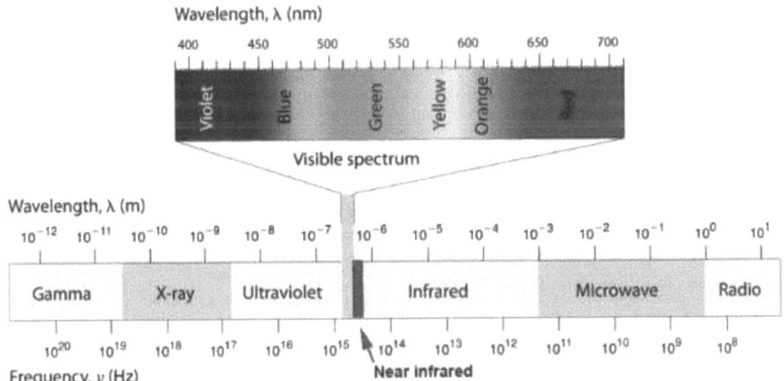

'Near'-infrared light is infrared light with a short wavelength.

4.4.1 PALM VEIN PATTERN RECOGNITION

The haemoglobin in your blood contains oxygen when it is transported from your lungs to the tissues in your body by your arteries. By the time the blood flows back to your heart via different arteries this oxygen has been released. Vein pattern recognition uses this difference between deoxidised and oxygenated haemoglobin. Deoxidised haemoglobin absorbs infrared light, making the vein pattern visible if you use a scanner to illuminate it with infrared light.

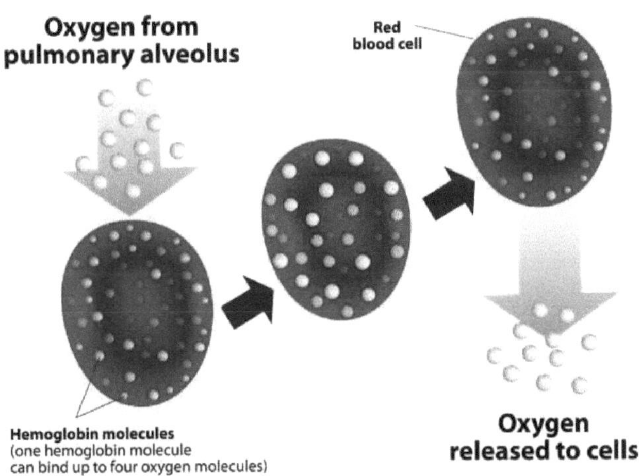

In the palm of their hand, everyone has a different vein pattern. As a result, the pattern's reference points can be saved, and the pattern can be used as an identification and protection technique. Most vein pattern recognition systems save the vein pattern as an image, which can be encoded or not. The scanned reference points, on the other hand, are explicitly stored as an encrypted tem with the Palm-ID.

4.4.2 FINGER VEIN PATTERN RECOGNITION

Finger vein pattern recognition is based on the same principle as palm vein pattern recognition. Illuminating the vein pattern in the fingers using near-infrared light makes it possible to discern this pattern, thanks to the deoxidised haemoglobin.

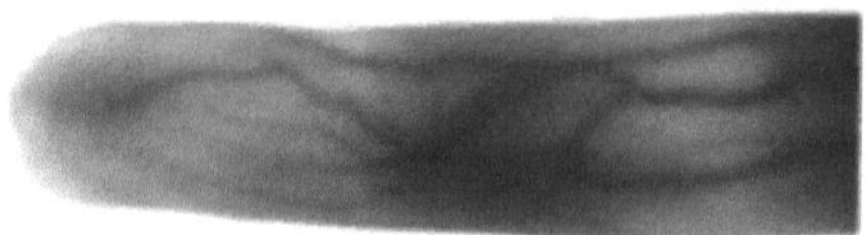

The surface area you're dealing with with a finger scan, on the other hand, is much smaller. On the one side, since the scanner is a smaller unit, this is a more portable technique than palm vein pattern recognition. However, since the finger must be placed more precisely on the scanner, it is less user-friendly. When it comes to vein pattern recognition, the more reference points there are, the greater the level of security and convenience that will be achieved.

4.4.3 RETINA VEIN PATTERN RECOGNITION

The human retina is a thin layer of tissue at the back of the eye. Because of the complex structure of capillaries that supply blood to the retina, every retina is unique.

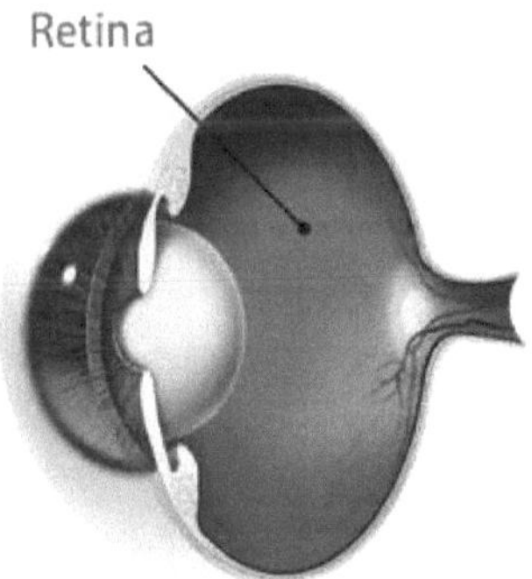

Scanning the retina with non-infrared light from the eyeball is used to recognise retina vein patterns. The vein pattern can be discerned and retained as an image since the blood vessels in the retina absorb this light. Since it is not a user-friendly technique, retina vein pattern recognition is becoming less common. Users must maintain mental composure in order for it to function properly.

UNIT-5

PERSON IDENTIFICATION APPROACHES

5.1 OVERVIEW

The customary human ID approaches rely upon alterable boundaries like passwords or attractive/ID cards. These boundaries can be effortlessly utilized by unlawful people, on the off chance that they know the secret word or have the card. Losing, neglecting, or taking are normal disservices for all the customary ID strategies which make it untrustworthy and incorrect particularly in the high exact framework like crime scene investigation, monetary, bank, and line ports frameworks. The requirement for more vigorous frameworks of individual recognizable proof notwithstanding the advancement of the sensors and computerized frameworks was motivator to build the frameworks that rely upon the special highlights of every individual. These highlights are removed from a human characteristic like finger impression, face, and discourse. Human acknowledgment utilizing highlights that are separated from inborn physical or conduct characteristics of the people is characterized as biometrics. Notwithstanding the upgrade of the productivity and capacity of acknowledgment frameworks, biometrics works with distinguishing, and guaranteeing measure, where it isn't needed to retain any passwords or to convey any ID cards like visas or driving permit.

Biometrics is the study of setting up the personality of an individual dependent on a vector of highlights got from a social qualities or explicit actual property that the individual holds. The conduct trademark incorporates how the individual associates and moves, like their talking style, hand signals, signature, and so forth The physiological classification incorporates the actual human attributes like fingerprints, iris, face, veins, eyes, hand shape, palmprint, and some more. Assessing these attributes helps the acknowledgment interaction utilizing the biometric frameworks.

A biometric framework incorporates two principle stages as enlistment and acknowledgment. Biometric information (picture, video, or discourse) are caught and put away in a data set in enlistment stage. The acknowledgment stage chiefly incorporates extraction of the remarkable highlights and age of the coordinating with scores to think about question highlights against the put away layouts. The biometric framework will report a character toward the finish of the choice cycle subsequent to performing coordinating, and this will be the personality of the most looking like individual in the data set.

5.2 COMMON BIOMETRIC TRIATS

In this section, a brief overview, requirements, advantages, and disadvantages of the most commonly used unimodal biometric traits are presented and explained.

5.2.1 FACE

Face acknowledgment is perhaps the main capacities that we use in our everyday lives. Face acknowledgment has been a functioning exploration territory in the course of the most recent 40 years, and the principal computerized face acknowledgment framework was created by Takeo Kanade in 1973 . The expanding interest in the face acknowledgment research is brought about by the palatable exhibition in numerous broadly utilized applications like the public security, business, and media information the executives applications that utilization face as biometric characteristic. Face acknowledgment enjoys a few upper hands over other biometrics, for example, unique finger impression and iris other than being common and nonintrusive. To begin with, the main benefit of face is that it tends to be caught a ways off and in undercover way. Second, notwithstanding the character, the face can likewise show the appearance and feeling of the individual like trouble, wonder, or startling. Besides, it gives a biographic information like sex and age. Third, enormous data sets of face pictures are now accessible, where the clients ought to give their face picture to gain driver's permit or ID card. At long last, individuals are for the most part more willing to share their face pictures in the public space as displayed by the expanding interest in web-based media applications (e.g., Facebook) with functionalities like face labelling.

A face acknowledgment framework for the most part comprises of four modules in particular face recognition, preprocessing, include extraction, and coordinating as demonstrated in Figure 5.1. A unique face picture and its preprocessed variation are likewise appeared in Figure 5.2.

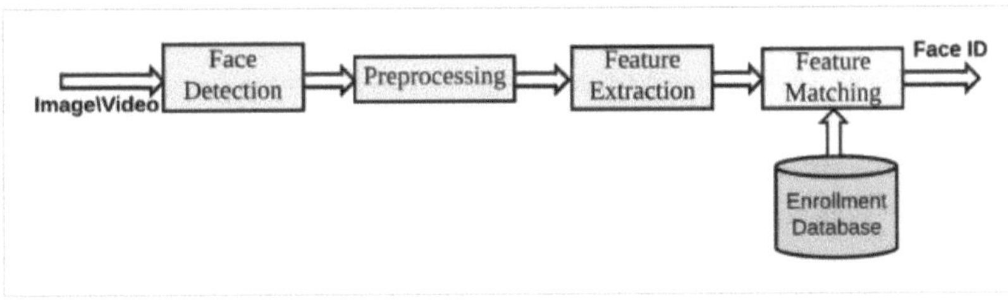

Figure 5.1 Block diagram of a face recognition system

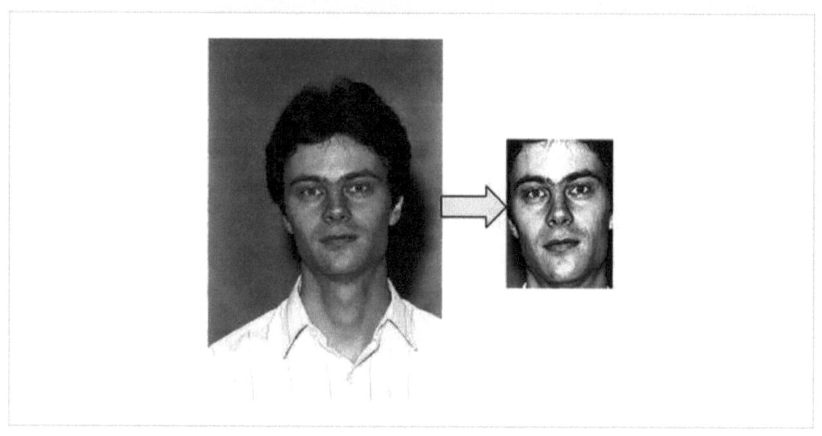

Figure 5.2 An original and a preprocessed face image.

5.2.2   IRIS

Iris acknowledgment is perhaps the most dependable techniques for individual ID. The utilization of iris surface investigation for biometric recognizable proof is plainly grounded with the benefits of uniqueness and strength. Iris acknowledgment has been effectively applied in access control frameworks overseeing huge data sets. The United Arab Emirates has been utilizing iris biometrics for line control and expellees following purposes for as far back as decade.

Iris is quite possibly the most significant attributes for programmed distinguishing proof of person. Various reasons legitimize this interest. As a matter of first importance, the iris is a secured inner organ of the eye that is noticeable from the outside. The iris is an annular construction and planar shape that turns effectively, and it has a rich surface. Moreover, iris surface is overwhelmingly a phenotypic with restricted hereditary penetrance. The appearance is steady over lifetime, which holds colossal guarantee for utilizing iris acknowledgment in assorted application situations, for example, line control, criminological examinations, and cryptosystems.

There are likewise a few disadvantages with it. It needs a lot of client collaboration for information procurement, and it is regularly touchy to impediment. Iris information procurement needs a controlled climate. Also, information procurement gadgets are very exorbitant. Iris acknowledgment can't be utilized in a clandestine circumstance.

A run of the mill iris acknowledgment framework has four unique modules like obtaining, division, standardization, and coordinating. These modules are appeared in Figure 3 for an overall iris acknowledgment framework.

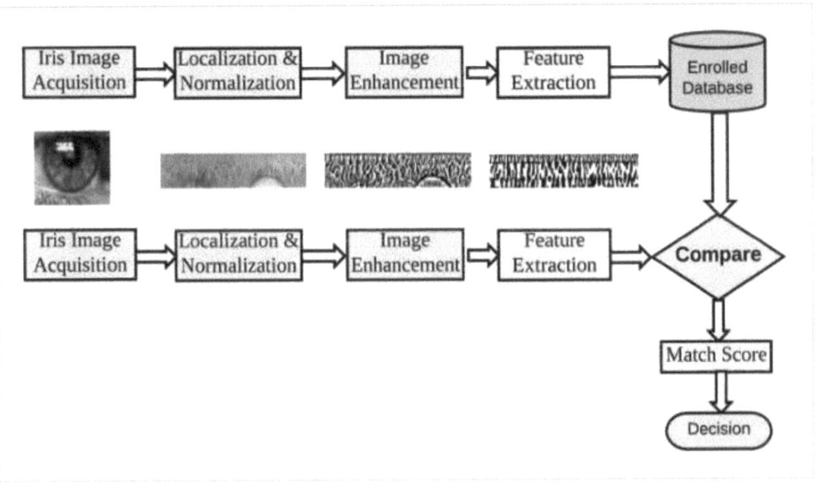

Figure 5.3 Block diagram of an iris recognition system.

5.2.3   PALM PRINT

The palmprint acknowledgment framework is considered as perhaps the best biometric frameworks that are solid and compelling. This framework recognizes the individual dependent on the chief lines, wrinkles, and edges on the outside of the palm. Studies and exploration more than 10 years have demonstrated that the intriguing component of palmprint is fixed and invariant, and a palmprint procured from any individual is one of a kind, so it tends to be dependable as a biometric quality.

A portion of the benefits of the palmprint acknowledgment contrasted and other biometric attribute frameworks are invariant line structure, low meddling, and the ease of catching gadget. Palmprint ID requires either high (alludes to 400 dpi or more) or low (alludes to 150 dpi or less) goal pictures in which high-goal pictures are reasonable for legal applications, for example, criminal recognition and low-goal pictures are more appropriate for common and business applications, for example, access control. High-goal and low-goal palmprint pictures are exhibited in Figure 4. Also,

34

the space of palmprint is bigger than unique finger impression; thus, there is a chance of catching more particular highlights in it.

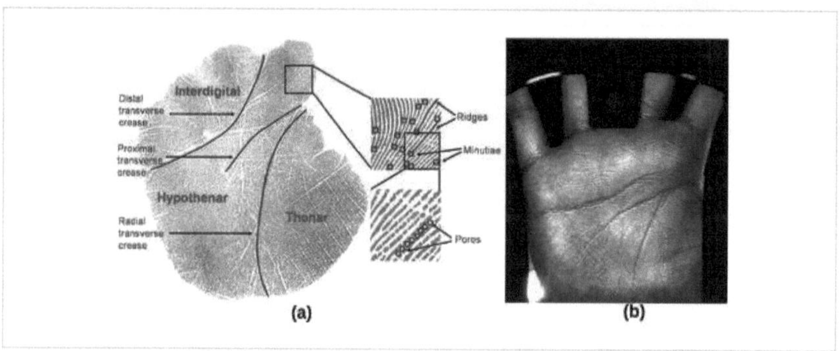

Figure 5.4 Palmprint features (a) a high-resolution image and (b) a low-resolution image.

Because of its minimal effort, easy to understand framework, high velocity, and high precision of palmprint acknowledgment, it tends to be considered as quite possibly the most solid and reasonable biometric acknowledgment framework. A ton of work has effectively been done about palmprint acknowledgment, since it is an intriguing exploration territory. Be that as it may, more exploration is expected to acquire productive palmprint framework.

There are three gatherings of imprints which are utilized in palmprint ID as mathematical highlights, line highlights (e.g., standard lines, wrinkles), and point highlights (e.g., particulars focuses). An ordinary palmprint acknowledgment framework comprises of palmprint procurement, preprocessing, include extraction, and coordinating with stages.

5.2.4　FINGER PRINT

The advanced history of unique finger impression recognizable proof starts in the nineteenth century with the improvement of ID agencies accused of keeping precise records about listed people. The procurement of unique finger impression was performed right off the bat by utilizing ink strategy.

The primary use of unique mark ID is legal examination of wrongdoings and played out a criminological distinguishing proof in the last part of the 1850s by planning a high-security ID framework that has consistently been the principle objective in the security business.

The primary explanations behind the ubiquity of finger impression acknowledgment are as per the following:

- The example of finger impression is interesting to every person and unchanging all through life from earliest stages to mature age and the examples of no two hands take after one another,

- Its accomplishment in different applications in the legal sciences, government, and non military personnel areas,

- The way that hoodlums frequently leave their fingerprints at crime locations,

- The presence of enormous inheritance data sets like National Institute of Standards and Technology (NIST), Fingerprint Verification Competition (FVC) assessment information bases from 2000, 2002, and 2004.

- The accessibility of minimal and moderately economical unique mark perusers.

An average finger impression include called particulars is extricated from finger impression pictures, as demonstrated in Figure 5.5, and utilized for coordinating with measure for a finger impression acknowledgment framework.

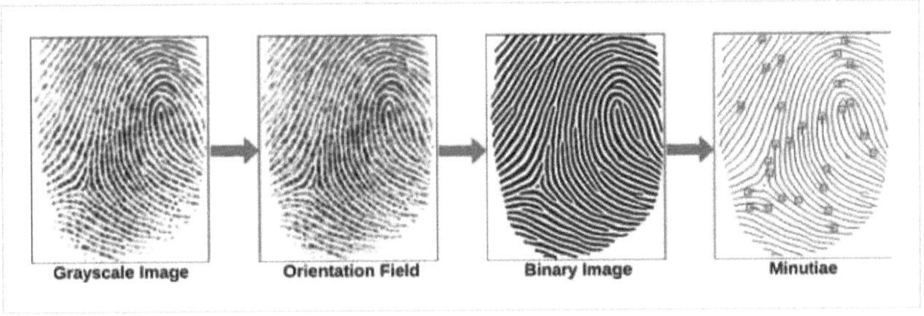

Figure 5.5 A typical minutiae feature extraction algorithm.

5.2.5   EAR

Perceiving individuals by their ear has as of late got huge consideration in the writing. There are numerous components that made ear a generally utilized biometrics. In the first place, the state of the ear and the design of cartilaginous tissue of the pinna are segregate. It is shaped by the external helix, the antihelix, the projection, the tragus, the antitragus, and the concha. The ear acknowledgment approaches depend on coordinating with the distance of notable focuses on the pinna from a milestone area. Second, ear has a design which doesn't differ with looks or time, and it is entirely steady for the finish of life. It has been shown that the acknowledgment rate isn't influenced by maturing. Third, ear biometric is advantageous as its securing is simple on the grounds that the size of the ear is bigger than unique mark, iris, and retina and more modest than face. Ear information can likewise be caught even without the information or participation of the client from far distance; accordingly, it very well may be utilized in inactive climate. This makes ear acknowledgment particularly fascinating for shrewd observation errands and for scientific picture investigation, since ear pictures can commonly be separated from profile head shots or video film.

The primary disadvantage of ear biometric is impediment, where the ear can be somewhat or completely covered by hair or by different things, for example, hood, amplifiers, adornments, or earphone. In a functioning ID framework, it's anything but a basic point as the subject can pull their hair back, yet in a latent recognizable proof, it is an issue as there will be no one educating the subject. Different difficulties on ears are various stances (points), left and right pivot, and diverse lighting conditions.

5.2.6   SPEECH

The exercises of programmed speaker check and recognizable proof have a long history returning to the mid-1960s. Mythical beast frameworks were the early applications that were utilized as discourse recognizer, which zeroed in on the capacity of acknowledgment framework to give acoustic information about speaker. Baum-Welch HMM techniques were utilized by these frameworks to prepare models.

Discourse or voice is one of the conduct attributes that can be utilized in biometric frameworks to distinguish the client dependent on the put away voice in the enlistment stage, where the voice qualities, for example, articulation style and voice surface are extraordinary and unmistakable for every individual. Then again, voice can likewise be viewed as physiological notwithstanding social component dependent on the state of the vocal track.

5.2.7   ADVANTAGES AND DISADVANTAGES OF VOICE RECOGNITION

For the most part, voice acknowledgment is nonintrusive, and individuals will acknowledge a discourse based biometric framework with as little bother as could really be expected. It additionally offers a modest acknowledgment innovation, since broadly useful voice recorders can be utilized to gain the information. Be that as it may, an individual's voice can be effectively recorded and can be utilized for approved admittance, and the commotion can be dropped by explicit programming. Accordingly, these make discourse acknowledgment to be utilized in numerous applications like monetary applications, security, retail, wrongdoing examination, diversion, and so forth Discourse based highlights are touchy to various factors, for example, foundation commotion, room resonation, the channel through which the discourse is procured, (for example, cell, land-line, and VoIP), covering discourse, and Lombard or hyper-enunciated discourse. Also, the passionate and actual condition of the speaker are significant. A disease, for example, influenza can change an individual's voice, and it makes voice acknowledgment troublesome. Discourse based confirmation is presently limited to low-security applications due to high inconstancy in a person's voice and helpless precision execution of an ordinary discourse based verification framework. Existing procedures can lessen changeability brought about by added substance clamor or direct twists, just as repaying gradually differing straight channels.

5.2.8   SPEECH RECOGNITION

Speech recognition measure begins by securing the sound from a client utilizing mouthpiece, and afterward, the arrangement of acoustic signs are changed over to a bunch of distinguishing words. The discourse acknowledgment relies upon numerous elements, for example, language model, jargon size, talking style, speaker enlistment, and transducer. Discourse acknowledgment framework is grouped to "speaker subordinate framework," if the client should prepare the framework prior to utilizing it, and to "speaker autonomous framework," if the framework can perceive any speaker's discourse without the need to prepare stage. Discourse acknowledgment frameworks can likewise be separated into "disconnected word discourse" or "constant discourse" in light of the quantity of the pre-owned vocabularies for ID measure.

Speaker models empower us to produce the scores from which we will decide. As in any example acknowledgment issue, the decisions are various, and the most famous and ruled procedure in most recent multi decade is Hidden Markov Models. There are likewise different strategies utilized for discourse acknowledgment frameworks like Artificial Neural Networks (ANN), Back Propagation Algorithm (BPA), Fast Fourier Transform (FFT), Learn Vector Quantization (LVQ), and Neural Networks (NN). An ordinary discourse acknowledgment framework is appeared in Figure 6.

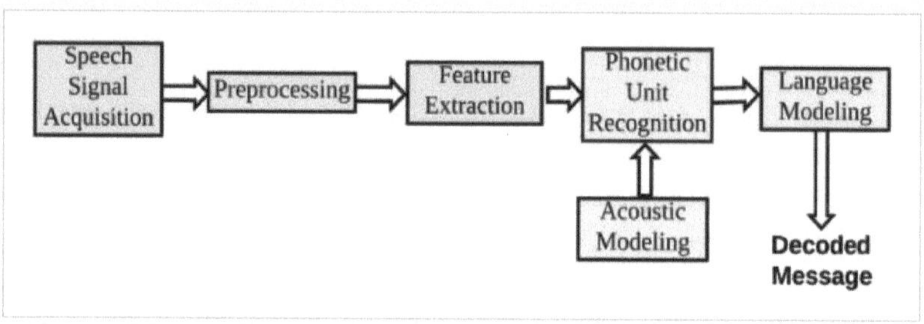

Figure 5.6. Block diagram of Speech recognition

5.2.9 PERFORMANCE EVALUATION

Different measurements can be used to evaluate the performance of biometric systems. The most famous measurement is the recognition rate, which is defined as the percentage of the samples that are correctly matched samples to the total tested samples. Another popular measurement is False Reject Rate (FRR) versus False Accept Rate (FAR) at various threshold values, where FRR refers to the expected probability for two mate samples which are wrongly mismatched and FAR refers to the expected probability that two non-mate samples are incorrectly matched.

Single-valued measure "Equal Error Rate (EER)," that is threshold independent, can also be used to evaluate the performance of recognition systems. EER is the value, where FRR and FAR are equal.

Detection Error Trade-off (DET) or Receiver Operating Characteristic (ROC) curves are also used to compare the performance of biometric systems in which both curves plot FRR against FAR in the normal deviate and linear scale, respectively.

5.2.10 DIMENSIONALITY OF INDEX KEY VECTOR

In biometric information ordering, a significant judgment is about the dimensionality of the file key vector. The dimensionality of the record vector ought to be in such a way that it diminishes the pursuit space essentially and simultaneously recovers a base number of up-and-comers without bargain in precision. In the accompanying, how this goal is accomplished regarding the diverse biometric information are summed up.

Greater part of the iris-based ordering methods consider the production of file key from iris surface. Among these surface based strategies, SIFT include based strategy gives the better outcome to the best of information. This technique utilizes 128-dimensional list key vector. As opposed to the current practices, this is the first run through iris biometric based ordering system is proposed utilizing Gabor energy highlights of iris surface. The Gabor energy highlights permit to infer just 12-dimensional list key for iris biometric. In reality this is very low component of file key vector in contrast with the few existing work. The synopsis of iris highlight portrayal is appeared in Table 5.7.

From the investigation of existing writing, it is seen that details based unique finger impression ordering utilizes low dimensional record key vector for finger impression information ordering. In addition, the MCC based unique finger impression ordering is treated as the most proficient particulars based ordering method. This strategy uses at any rate 15 dimensional record key vector. Then again, the element extraction strategy utilizing two nearest point triangulation technique creates 8-dimensional list key vectors. To add more, the scale and revolution invariant properties of file keys make the proposed ordering plan more vigorous contrasted with other higher dimensional file key vector detailed somewhere else. Table 5.7 shows the outline of unique mark highlights.

To accomplish the improved precision of the ordering framework, the current face biometric information ordering procedures advocate high dimensional record key vector. As indicated by the revealed work, it is seen that the technique proposed gives better exactness. This strategy utilizes 128-dimensional record key vectors. Conversely, the proposed face biometric information ordering system considers 69-dimensional list key vectors. It could be noticed that in the proposed 69-dimensional face ordering system, the initial four components of the record key vector are comprised from the central issue.

Indexing method	Feature representation	
	Features	Dimensions
Iris	Gabor energy features	12
Fingerprint	Geometric and Gabor energy features extracted from two-closest point triangles	8
Face	SURF key points and descriptors	69
Multimodal	Relative scores	4

Information, which are used to index the face data. The next 64 dimensions, which contain the SURF feature descriptors information, are used to match the face template. The last dimension of the index key vector is the identity of a subject. The summary of face feature are reported in Table 5.1.

5.2.11 STORING AND RETRIEVING

Capacity structure is another significant issue in any ordering instrument. It could be noticed that capacity construction ought to shift contingent upon the file key and the information structure likewise exceptionally impacts the recovering productivity. Further, ordering procedure needs additional memory overhead. The examination to accomplish the best stockpiling structure for the ordering of iris, finger impression, face and multimodal biometric information are talked about in the accompanying.

Existing iris information ordering procedures utilize distinctive putting away constructions which are more applicable to the conventional recovery strategies. The tree-based capacity structure is regularly used to store the iris information. Albeit, the recovering proficiency in tree-based putting away may not be satisfactory for an enormous number of passages into the data set. Despite what is generally expected, table-based capacity structure is utilized in the proposed iris ordering method. A table is kept up for an element of the iris file key vector and put away all iris information into the table dependent on the worth of that measurement in the record space. This proposed stockpiling structure assists with recovering a little arrangement of applicants from the data set in steady time utilizing the proposed recovering instrument. Further, the low dimensionality of the list key vector decreases the memory overhead for the iris ordering framework.

From the current writing, it tends to be seen that dominant part of the unique finger impression ordering approaches follow consistent grouping system and for this reason they utilize direct capacity structure. Then again, to store the finger impression information, three diverse putting away constructions: straight, bunched and grouped kd-tree are utilized. In the finger impression ordering approach, k-implies grouping strategy is applied on record keys to bunch the finger impression information. Three hunt strategies are tested for these three putting away constructions. It is seen that grouped and bunched kd-tree look effectively decrease the pursuit space of finger impression information. The proposed approach manages low dimensional record key vector, thus, less ordering memory overhead is required. By the by, the grouped kd-tree based capacity requires an additional memory overhead to store the bunch and kd-tree data.

Existing face ordering strategies barely investigate the putting away designs of the face-based listed information. In the proposed face ordering, biometric information are put away into a two level record space in the data set. In the main level, the face information are separated into two gatherings dependent on the principal measurement of the file keys and in second level, a 3-dimensional record shape is made dependent on the following three components of the list keys. A straight or kd-tree structure is utilized inside a cell of a file shape to store the face information. A hash work is applied on the file keys to store and recover the face information. The proposed putting away and recovering strategies permit to proficiently create an exact applicant set with comparative layout for a given inquiry. Be that as it may, the proposed putting away method needs a little memory to store the two level file space into the data set as just four components of the file key vector are utilized to make the file space.

5.2.12 THREATS TO VALIDITY

Internal Validity:-

Capacity structure is another significant issue in any ordering instrument. It could be noticed that capacity construction ought to shift contingent upon the file key and the information structure likewise exceptionally impacts the recovering productivity. Further, ordering procedure needs additional memory overhead. The examination to accomplish the best stockpiling structure for the ordering of iris, finger impression, face and multimodal biometric information are talked about in the accompanying.

Existing iris information ordering procedures utilize distinctive putting away constructions which are more applicable to the conventional recovery strategies. The tree-based capacity structure is regularly used to store the iris information. Albeit, the recovering proficiency in tree-based putting away may not be satisfactory for an enormous number of passages into the data set. Despite what is generally expected, table-based capacity structure is utilized in the proposed iris ordering method. A table is kept up for an element of the iris file key vector and put away all iris information into the table dependent on the worth of that measurement in the record space. This proposed stockpiling structure assists with recovering a little arrangement of applicants from the data set in steady time utilizing the proposed recovering instrument. Further, the low dimensionality of the list key vector decreases the memory overhead for the iris ordering framework.

From the current writing, it tends to be seen that dominant part of the unique finger impression ordering approaches follow consistent grouping system and for this reason they utilize direct capacity structure. Then again, to store the finger impression information, three diverse putting away constructions: straight, bunched and grouped kd-tree are utilized. In the finger impression ordering approach, k-implies grouping strategy is applied on record keys to bunch the finger impression information. Three hunt strategies are tested for these three putting away constructions. It is seen that grouped and bunched kd-tree look effectively decrease the pursuit space of finger impression information. The proposed approach manages low dimensional record key vector, thus, less ordering memory overhead is required. By the by, the grouped kd-tree based capacity requires an additional memory overhead to store the bunch and kd-tree data.

Existing face ordering strategies barely investigate the putting away designs of the face-based listed information. In the proposed face ordering, biometric information are put away into a two level record space in the data set. In the main level, the face information are separated into two gatherings dependent on the principal measurement of the file keys and in second level, a 3-dimensional record shape is made dependent on the following three components of the list keys. A straight or kd-tree structure is utilized inside a cell of a file shape to store the face information. A hash work is applied on the file keys to store and recover the face information. The proposed putting away and recovering strategies permit to proficiently create an exact applicant set with comparative layout for a given inquiry. Be that as it may, the proposed putting away method needs a little memory to store the two level file space into the data set as just four components of the file key vector are utilized to make the file space.

External Validity

The elements which may restrict the speculation of exploratory outcomes have been approved here. The entirety of the proposed unimodal ordering strategies are tried with the diverse unimodal information bases (BATH, CASIAV3I, CASIAV4T, MMU2 and WVU iris data set for iris biometric ordering, NIST DB4, NIST DB4 Natural and FVC 2004 finger impression data sets for finger impression ordering, and FERET and FRGC data set for face biometric ordering) with moderate size which are accessible for the exploration networks. The vast majority of these information bases are made in controlled test arrangement. In this way, it ought not be asserted the outcomes pertinent to a biometric data sets. Additionally, to set up the outcomes it should be approved with different data sets, which couldn't be gotten to during the analyses. Further, the size of the data sets are in the request for thousands. Subsequently, the utilization of exceptionally huge size information bases which are in the request for millions may marginally influence the exhibition of the proposed approaches. Just the front facing face pictures are considered in face biometric based ordering framework. Subsequently, aftereffects of face biometric ordering might be influenced for the other face profiles (left face profile, right face profile, and so on) and blocked face pictures as the element extraction is troublesome from these kinds of pictures. Further, the proposed multimodal biometric ordering strategy is satisfactorily tried with the virtual clients' data set. Thus, it ought not be guaranteed that the presentation of the proposed multimodal ordering will stay same for the clients' data set with genuine multibiometric information.

REFERENCES:

[1] H. Bay, A. Ess, T. Tuytelaars, and L. V. Gool. SURF: Speeded Up Robust Features. Computer Vision and Image Understanding , 110(3):346–359, 2008. doi: http://dx.doi.org/10.1016/j.cviu. 2007.09.014.

[2] B. Bhanu and X. Tan. Fingerprint Indexing Bsed on Novel Features of Minutiae Triplets. IEEE Transactions on Pattern Analysis and Machine Intelligence, 25(5):616–622, 2003. ISSN 0162-8828.

[3] R. Cappelli. Fast and Accurate Fingerprint Indexing Based on Ridge Orientation and Frequency. IEEE Transactions on Systems, Man, and Cybernetics, Part B: Cybernetics, 41(6):1511–1521, 2011.

[4] R. Cappelli, M. Ferrara, and D. Maltoni. Fingerprint Indexing Based on Minutia Cylinder-Code. IEEE Transactions on Pattern Analysis and Machine Intelligence, 33(5):1051–1057, 2011.

[5] J. Daugman. The Importance of being Random: Statistical Principles of Iris Recognition. Pattern Recognition, 36(2):279–291, 2003.

[6] J. Daugman. How Iris Recognition Works. IEEE Transactions on Circuits and Systems for Video Technology, 14(1):21–30, 2004.

[7] G. Du, F. Su, and A. Cai. Face Recognition using SURF Features. In Proceedings of the SPIE Pattern Recognition and Computer Vision (MIPPR 2009), volume SPIE-7496, pages 749628–1– 749628–7, Yichang, China, October-November 2009.

[8] A. Gyaourova and A. Ross. A Novel Coding Scheme for Indexing Fingerprint Patterns. In Proceedings of the 7th International Workshop Statistical Pattern Recognition, pages 755–764, Orlando, USA, December 2008.

[9] Aglika Gyaourova and Arun Ross. Index Codes for Multibiometric Pattern Retrieval. IEEE Transactions on Information Forensics and Security, 7(2):518–529, 2012.

[10] L. Hong, Y. Wan, and A. Jain. Fingerprint Image Enhancement: Algorithm and Performance Evaluation. IEEE Transactions on Pattern Analysis and Machine Intelligence, 20(8):777–789, 1998. ISSN 0162-8828.

Printed by Books on Demand GmbH, Norderstedt / Germany